Shelley Jade

A Complete G Hysterectomy Recovery and Cooking

Delicious and Nutrient-Packed Dishes for Pre-Op Strength and Post-Op Recovery

BY

SHELLEY JADE

Copyright@2024 Shelley Jade

All Rights Reserved

TABLE OF CONTENTS

Introduction 4

CHAPTER 1 9

Understanding Nutritional Needs Before Hysterectomy 9

CHAPTER 2 14

Pre-Operative Recipes 14

CHAPTER 3 95

Importance of post-operative nutrition 95

CHAPTER 4 122

Post-Operative Recipe Collection 122

CHAPTER 5 182

Building a Post-Hysterectomy Diet Plan 182

Conclusion 190

Introduction

Welcome to "A Complete Guide to Hysterectomy Recovery and Cooking" In the journey of a woman's life, certain moments demand not only physical strength but also a nourished spirit. The decision to undergo a hysterectomy is one such pivotal moment. We understand that this journey is unique, transformative, and deserves a companion that supports not just recovery but empowers a holistic well-being.

The purpose of this cookbook extends beyond a collection of recipes. It is a culinary guide meticulously crafted for the distinctive phases of a hysterectomy – both before and after. The goal is to provide a valuable resource that enhances your journey, bringing together the healing power of nutrition, the joy of cooking, and the strength derived from a community of women who have walked a similar path.

The Role of Nutrition in Pre and Post-Hysterectomy Care

Proper nutrition plays a crucial role in both pre and post-hysterectomy care. Before undergoing a hysterectomy, it is important to focus on maintaining a healthy diet to support overall well-being and prepare the body for surgery. This includes consuming a balanced diet rich in fruits, vegetables, whole grains, lean proteins, and healthy fats.

During the pre-hysterectomy phase, it is beneficial to incorporate foods that are known to promote healing and reduce inflammation. These may include foods high in antioxidants, such as berries, leafy greens, and nuts. Additionally, foods rich in iron, such as lean meats, beans, and fortified cereals, can help prevent anemia, which is a common concern before surgery.

After a hysterectomy, proper nutrition becomes even more important for a smooth recovery. It is essential to focus on foods that support wound healing, boost energy levels, and promote overall health. Adequate protein intake is crucial for tissue repair, so incorporating lean meats, fish, eggs, dairy products, or plant-based protein sources like legumes and tofu is recommended.

Foods high in fiber, such as whole grains, fruits, and vegetables, can help prevent constipation, which is a common side effect of surgery and certain medications. Staying hydrated is also important, so drinking plenty of water throughout the day is essential.

It is important to consult with a healthcare professional or a registered dietitian for personalized nutrition advice tailored to your specific needs and medical history. They can provide guidance on portion sizes, specific dietary restrictions, and any supplements that may be necessary.

Remember, nutrition is a vital component of pre and post-hysterectomy care, and making healthy food choices can contribute to a smoother recovery and overall well-being.

CHAPTER 1

Understanding Nutritional Needs Before Hysterectomy

Understanding your nutritional needs before a hysterectomy is important for preparing your body for surgery and promoting optimal healing and recovery.

1. Consult with your healthcare provider: It is crucial to consult with your healthcare provider before undergoing any surgery, including a hysterectomy. They will provide you with specific instructions tailored to your individual needs.

2. Maintain a healthy diet: Eating a balanced and nutritious diet can help support your body's healing process. Include plenty of fruits, vegetables, whole grains, and lean proteins in your meals. Avoid excessive consumption of processed foods, sugary snacks, and unhealthy fats.

3. Stay hydrated: Proper hydration is essential for your overall health and recovery. Drink plenty of water throughout the day and limit your intake of caffeinated and sugary beverages.

4. Quit smoking and limit alcohol consumption: Smoking can interfere with the healing process and increase the risk of complications. It is

advisable to quit smoking before surgery. Additionally, limit your alcohol consumption as it can negatively impact your body's ability to heal.

5. Manage stress: Stress can have a negative impact on your body's ability to heal. Engage in stress-reducing activities such as meditation, deep breathing exercises, or engaging in hobbies you enjoy.

Foods That Support Healing

In the realm of post-operative recovery, the significance of a well-balanced and nutrient-rich diet cannot be overstated. As you navigate the path towards healing after a hysterectomy, the foods you choose become crucial agents in your recovery process. Here are some suggestions:

1. Lean Proteins: Include sources of lean proteins like chicken, turkey, fish, tofu, and legumes. These foods provide essential amino acids for tissue repair and help in building strength.

2. Colorful Fruits and Vegetables: Incorporate a variety of colorful fruits and vegetables into your recipes. They are rich in antioxidants, vitamins, and minerals that support the healing process and boost the immune system.

3. Whole Grains: Opt for whole grains like quinoa, brown rice, oats, and whole wheat bread.

These foods provide fiber, which aids in digestion and helps prevent constipation, a common issue after surgery.

4. Healthy Fats: Include sources of healthy fats such as avocados, nuts, seeds, and olive oil. These fats provide essential nutrients and help reduce inflammation in the body.

5. Fermented Foods: Consider adding fermented foods like yogurt, kefir, sauerkraut, and kimchi to your recipes. They contain beneficial probiotics that support gut health and aid in digestion.

6. Herbal Teas: Include herbal teas like chamomile, ginger, and peppermint. They can help soothe the digestive system and promote relaxation.

CHAPTER 2

Pre-Operative Recipes

Pre-operative recipes are meals or dishes that are specifically designed to be consumed before a surgical procedure, such as a hysterectomy. These recipes are often focused on providing the body with essential nutrients, vitamins, and minerals to help prepare it for the upcoming surgery. They can also help to optimize the body's healing process and reduce the risk of complications. In the realm of preparing for a hysterectomy, the importance of pre-operative nutrition cannot be overstated.

Energizing Breakfast Options

Mornings are a crucial part of your day, setting the tone for what follows. As you navigate the path toward a hysterectomy, ensuring your mornings begin with nourishing and energizing breakfast options becomes paramount.

Here are some recipes designed to fortify your body and prepare you for a hysterectomy.

Energizing Berry Smoothie

Ingredients:

- 1 cup frozen mixed berries (such as strawberries, blueberries, and raspberries)

- 1 ripe banana

- 1/2 cup almond milk (or any other milk of your choice)

- 1 tablespoon honey or maple syrup (optional, for sweetness)

- Toppings of your choice (such as granola, sliced fruits, chia seeds, coconut flakes, etc.)

Instructions:

1. In a blender, add the frozen mixed berries, ripe banana, almond milk, and honey or maple syrup (if using).

2. Blend the ingredients until smooth and creamy. If the mixture is too thick, you can add a little more almond milk to achieve the desired consistency.

3. Once the smoothie is ready, pour it into a bowl.

4. Now it's time to add your favorite toppings! You can sprinkle some granola, sliced fruits, chia seeds, coconut flakes, or any other toppings you prefer.

5. Enjoy your energizing berry smoothie bowl right away!

Spinach and Feta Omelette:

Ingredients:

- 3 large eggs

- 1/4 cup fresh spinach, chopped

- 1/4 cup crumbled feta cheese

- Salt and pepper to taste

- 1 tablespoon olive oil or butter

Instructions:

1. Crack the eggs into a bowl and whisk them until well beaten. Season with salt and pepper.

2. Heat the olive oil or butter in a non-stick skillet over medium heat.

3. Add the chopped spinach to the skillet and sauté for about 1-2 minutes until wilted.

4. Pour the beaten eggs into the skillet, making sure they cover the entire surface.

5. Allow the eggs to cook undisturbed for a few minutes until the edges start to set.

6. Sprinkle the crumbled feta cheese evenly over one half of the omelette.

7. Using a spatula, carefully fold the other half of the omelette over the cheese side.

8. Cook for another minute or so until the cheese melts and the omelette is cooked through.

9. Slide the omelette onto a plate and serve hot.

Avocado toast with poached egg

Ingredients:

- 1 ripe avocado

- 2 slices of bread (whole wheat or your preferred type)

- 2 eggs

- Salt and pepper to taste

- Optional toppings: red pepper flakes, sliced tomatoes, feta cheese, or fresh herbs like cilantro or parsley

Instructions:

1. Start by toasting the bread slices to your desired level of crispiness.

2. While the bread is toasting, cut the avocado in half and remove the pit. Scoop out the flesh into a bowl and mash it with a fork until it reaches your desired consistency.

3. Season the mashed avocado with salt and pepper to taste.

4. In a separate pot, bring water to a gentle simmer. Add a splash of vinegar to the water (optional) to help the eggs hold their shape.

5. Crack one egg into a small bowl or ramekin. Create a gentle whirlpool in the simmering water using a spoon, then carefully slide the egg into the center of the whirlpool. Repeat with the second egg.

6. Allow the eggs to poach for about 3-4 minutes, or until the whites are set but the yolks are still

runny. Adjust the cooking time based on your preference for yolk consistency.

7. While the eggs are poaching, spread the mashed avocado evenly onto the toasted bread slices.

8. Once the eggs are done, carefully remove them from the water using a slotted spoon and place them on top of the avocado toast.

9. Sprinkle with additional salt, pepper, and any optional toppings you desire.

10. Serve immediately and enjoy your delicious avocado toast with poached egg!

Quinoa Breakfast Bowl:

Ingredients:

- 1 cup cooked quinoa

- 1/2 cup Greek yogurt

- 1/4 cup fresh berries (such as strawberries, blueberries, or raspberries)

- 1 tablespoon honey or maple syrup

- 1 tablespoon chia seeds

- 1 tablespoon nuts or seeds (such as almonds, walnuts, or pumpkin seeds)

- Optional toppings: sliced banana, shredded coconut, or granola

Instructions:

1. Start by cooking the quinoa according to the package instructions. Once cooked, let it cool slightly.

2. In a bowl, combine the cooked quinoa, Greek yogurt, fresh berries, honey or maple syrup, chia seeds, and nuts or seeds.

3. Mix everything together until well combined.

4. If desired, add additional toppings such as sliced banana, shredded coconut, or granola.

5. Serve immediately and enjoy your nutritious and delicious Quinoa Breakfast Bowl!

Greek Yogurt Parfait:

Ingredients:

- 1 cup of Greek yogurt

- 1/2 cup of granola

- 1/2 cup of mixed berries (such as strawberries, blueberries, and raspberries)

- 1 tablespoon of honey (optional)

- 1/4 cup of chopped nuts (such as almonds or walnuts) (optional)

Instructions:

1. In a glass or a bowl, start by layering half of the Greek yogurt at the bottom.

2. Add a layer of granola on top of the yogurt.

3. Next, add a layer of mixed berries on top of the granola.

4. Repeat the layers with the remaining Greek yogurt, granola, and mixed berries.

5. Drizzle honey on top for added sweetness (optional).

6. Sprinkle chopped nuts on top for added crunch (optional).

7. Serve immediately and enjoy your Greek Yogurt Parfait!

Sweet Potato and Kale Hash:

Ingredients:

- 2 medium sweet potatoes, peeled and diced

- 1 bunch of kale, stems removed and leaves chopped

- 1 onion, diced

- 2 cloves of garlic, minced

- 2 tablespoons of olive oil

- Salt and pepper to taste

- Optional toppings: fried eggs, avocado slices, hot sauce

Instructions:

1. Heat the olive oil in a large skillet over medium heat.

2. Add the diced sweet potatoes to the skillet and cook for about 5 minutes, stirring occasionally, until they start to soften.

3. Add the diced onion and minced garlic to the skillet and cook for another 3-4 minutes, until the onion becomes translucent.

4. Add the chopped kale to the skillet and cook for about 5 minutes, until it wilts and becomes tender.

5. Season with salt and pepper to taste.

6. Remove from heat and serve the Sweet Potato and Kale Hash hot.

7. You can top it with fried eggs, avocado slices, or hot sauce if desired.

Chia seed pudding

Ingredients:

- 1/4 cup chia seeds

- 1 cup milk (you can use any type of milk - dairy or plant-based)

- Sweetener of your choice (such as honey, maple syrup, or stevia)

- Optional toppings (such as fresh fruits, nuts, or coconut flakes)

Instructions:

1. In a bowl, combine the chia seeds and milk. Stir well to make sure the chia seeds are evenly distributed.

2. Let the mixture sit for about 5 minutes, then stir again to prevent clumping.

3. Cover the bowl and refrigerate for at least 2 hours or overnight. This will allow the chia seeds to absorb the liquid and create a pudding-like consistency.

4. After the pudding has set, give it a good stir to break up any clumps.

5. Taste the pudding and add sweetener to your liking. Start with a small amount and adjust as needed.

6. Serve the chia seed pudding in individual bowls or jars.

7. If desired, top the pudding with your favorite toppings, such as fresh fruits, nuts, or coconut flakes.

8. Enjoy your homemade chia seed pudding!

Whole grain pancakes with blueberry compote:

Ingredients:

For the pancakes:

- 1 cup whole wheat flour

- 1 tablespoon baking powder

- 1 tablespoon sugar

- 1/4 teaspoon salt

- 1 cup milk (dairy or plant-based)

- 1 egg

- 2 tablespoons melted butter or oil

For the blueberry compote:

- 1 cup fresh or frozen blueberries

- 2 tablespoons sugar

- 1 tablespoon lemon juice

- 1/4 cup water

Instructions:

For the pancakes:

1. In a large bowl, whisk together the whole wheat flour, baking powder, sugar, and salt.

2. In a separate bowl, whisk together the milk, egg, and melted butter or oil.

3. Pour the wet ingredients into the dry ingredients and stir until just combined. Be careful not to overmix, as this can make the pancakes tough.

4. Heat a non-stick skillet or griddle over medium heat. Grease the surface with a little butter or oil.

5. Pour 1/4 cup of batter onto the skillet for each pancake. Cook until bubbles form on the surface, then flip and cook for another 1-2 minutes, or until golden brown.

6. Repeat with the remaining batter, adding more butter or oil to the skillet as needed.

For the blueberry compote:

1. In a small saucepan, combine the blueberries, sugar, lemon juice, and water.

2. Bring the mixture to a simmer over medium heat, stirring occasionally.

3. Cook for about 5-7 minutes, or until the blueberries have softened and the mixture has thickened slightly.

4. Remove from heat and let the compote cool slightly before serving.

To serve:

1. Stack the pancakes on a plate and top with the blueberry compote.

2. You can also add additional toppings like a dollop of yogurt or a sprinkle of powdered sugar if desired.

Turmeric and Ginger Smoothie.

Ingredients:

- 1 cup of unsweetened almond milk (or any other milk of your choice)

- 1 ripe banana

- 1 teaspoon of turmeric powder

- 1 teaspoon of grated ginger

- 1 tablespoon of honey (optional, for sweetness)

- 1 tablespoon of chia seeds (optional, for added nutrition)

- A pinch of black pepper (optional, helps with turmeric absorption)

- Ice cubes (optional, for a chilled smoothie)

Instructions:

1. Peel the banana and break it into smaller pieces.

2. In a blender, add the almond milk, banana pieces, turmeric powder, grated ginger, honey (if using), chia seeds (if using), and black pepper (if using).

3. Blend everything together until smooth and creamy.

4. If you prefer a colder smoothie, you can add a few ice cubes and blend again until well combined.

5. Once the smoothie reaches your desired consistency, pour it into a glass and enjoy!

Mango and Coconut Chia Pudding.

Ingredients:

- 1 ripe mango

- 1 cup of coconut milk

- 1/4 cup of chia seeds

- 1 tablespoon of honey or maple syrup (optional, for sweetness)

- A pinch of salt

Instructions:

1. Peel the mango and remove the flesh from the pit. Cut the mango into small pieces.

2. In a blender, add the mango pieces and coconut milk. Blend until smooth and creamy.

3. In a bowl, combine the mango-coconut mixture, chia seeds, honey or maple syrup (if using), and a pinch of salt. Stir well to combine.

4. Cover the bowl and refrigerate for at least 4 hours or overnight. This allows the chia seeds to absorb the liquid and create a pudding-like consistency.

5. After the pudding has set, give it a good stir to make sure the chia seeds are evenly distributed.

6. Serve the mango and coconut chia pudding chilled, and you can top it with additional mango slices or shredded coconut if desired.

Light and Nourishing Lunch Ideas

In the transformative journey of a hysterectomy, nourishing your body with wholesome and satisfying meals becomes an integral part of self-care. This section of this cookbook is dedicated to light and nourishing lunch ideas designed to bring both flavor and vitality to your plate. Here are some recipes designed to fortify your body and prepare you for a hysterectomy.

Quinoa and Vegetable Salad.

Ingredients:

- 1 cup quinoa

- 2 cups water or vegetable broth

- 1 cup diced vegetables (such as bell peppers, cucumbers, cherry tomatoes, carrots, etc.)

- 1/4 cup chopped fresh herbs (such as parsley, cilantro, or basil)

- 1/4 cup crumbled feta cheese (optional)

- 2 tablespoons olive oil

- 2 tablespoons lemon juice

- Salt and pepper to taste

Instructions:

1. Rinse the quinoa under cold water to remove any bitterness.

2. In a medium-sized saucepan, bring the water or vegetable broth to a boil. Add the rinsed quinoa and reduce the heat to low. Cover and simmer for

about 15-20 minutes, or until the quinoa is cooked and the liquid is absorbed.

3. Once cooked, remove the quinoa from the heat and let it cool for a few minutes.

4. In a large bowl, combine the cooked quinoa, diced vegetables, chopped herbs, and crumbled feta cheese (if using).

5. In a small bowl, whisk together the olive oil, lemon juice, salt, and pepper. Pour the dressing over the quinoa and vegetable mixture.

6. Toss everything together until well combined and evenly coated with the dressing.

7. Taste and adjust the seasoning if needed.

8. Serve the quinoa and vegetable salad chilled or at room temperature.

Avocado and Chickpea Wrap

Ingredients:

- 1 ripe avocado, mashed

- 1 can chickpeas, drained and rinsed

- 1/4 cup diced red onion

- 1/4 cup diced bell peppers

- 1/4 cup diced cucumber

- 1/4 cup chopped fresh cilantro

- Juice of 1 lime

- Salt and pepper to taste

- Tortilla wraps

Instructions:

1. In a medium-sized bowl, mash the avocado with a fork until smooth.

2. Add the drained and rinsed chickpeas to the bowl and roughly mash them with a fork or potato masher. Leave some chickpeas whole for texture.

3. Add the diced red onion, bell peppers, cucumber, and chopped cilantro to the bowl. Mix everything together.

4. Squeeze the juice of 1 lime over the mixture and season with salt and pepper to taste. Mix well to combine all the flavors.

5. Lay a tortilla wrap flat on a clean surface. Spoon a generous amount of the avocado and chickpea mixture onto the center of the tortilla.

6. Fold the sides of the tortilla inward, then roll it up tightly from the bottom to create a wrap.

7. Repeat with the remaining tortilla wraps and filling.

8. Serve the avocado and chickpea wraps immediately, or you can wrap them in foil and refrigerate for later.

Mango and Shrimp Salad:

Ingredients:

- 1 pound of cooked shrimp, peeled and deveined

- 2 ripe mangoes, peeled and diced

- 1 red bell pepper, diced

- 1/2 red onion, thinly sliced

- 1/4 cup fresh cilantro, chopped

- Juice of 2 limes

- 2 tablespoons olive oil

- Salt and pepper to taste.

Instructions:

1. In a large bowl, combine the cooked shrimp, diced mangoes, diced red bell pepper, thinly sliced red onion, and chopped cilantro.

2. In a separate small bowl, whisk together the lime juice, olive oil, salt, and pepper.

3. Pour the dressing over the shrimp and mango mixture, and gently toss to combine.

4. Let the salad marinate in the refrigerator for at least 30 minutes to allow the flavors to meld together.

5. Serve chilled and enjoy!

Lemon Garlic Chicken Quinoa Bowl:

Ingredients:

- 2 boneless, skinless chicken breasts

- 1 cup quinoa

- 2 cups chicken broth

- 2 tablespoons olive oil

- 4 cloves garlic, minced

- Juice of 1 lemon

- 1 teaspoon dried oregano

- Salt and pepper to taste

- 1 cucumber, diced

- 1 cup cherry tomatoes, halved

- 1/4 cup red onion, thinly sliced

- 1/4 cup fresh parsley, chopped

Instructions:

1. Preheat your oven to 400°F (200°C).

2. Season the chicken breasts with salt, pepper, and dried oregano.

3. In a large oven-safe skillet, heat 1 tablespoon of olive oil over medium-high heat. Add the chicken breasts and cook for about 4-5 minutes on each side until browned.

4. Transfer the skillet to the preheated oven and bake for about 15-20 minutes or until the chicken is cooked through and no longer pink in the center. Remove from the oven and let it rest for a few minutes before slicing.

5. While the chicken is cooking, rinse the quinoa under cold water. In a medium saucepan, bring the chicken broth to a boil. Add the rinsed quinoa, reduce the heat to low, cover, and simmer for about 15 minutes or until the quinoa is cooked and the liquid is absorbed. Fluff the quinoa with a fork.

6. In a small bowl, whisk together the minced garlic, lemon juice, remaining tablespoon of olive oil, salt, and pepper.

7. In a large bowl, combine the cooked quinoa, diced cucumber, halved cherry tomatoes, thinly sliced red onion, and chopped parsley. Pour the lemon garlic dressing over the quinoa mixture and toss to combine.

8. Slice the cooked chicken breasts and serve on top of the quinoa salad.

9. Enjoy your Lemon Garlic Chicken Quinoa Bowl!

Caprese Stuffed Portobello Mushrooms.

Ingredients:

- 4 large Portobello mushrooms

- 2 tablespoons olive oil

- 2 cloves garlic, minced

- 1 cup cherry tomatoes, halved

- 8 ounces fresh mozzarella cheese, sliced

- 1/4 cup fresh basil leaves, chopped

- Balsamic glaze, for drizzling

- Salt and pepper, to taste

Instructions:

1. Preheat your oven to 400°F (200°C). Line a baking sheet with parchment paper.

2. Clean the Portobello mushrooms by gently wiping them with a damp cloth. Remove the stems and scrape out the gills using a spoon.

3. In a small bowl, mix together the olive oil and minced garlic. Brush the mixture onto both sides of the mushrooms.

4. Place the mushrooms on the prepared baking sheet, gill side up. Season with salt and pepper.

5. Divide the cherry tomato halves evenly among the mushrooms, placing them in the gill area.

6. Top each mushroom with slices of fresh mozzarella cheese.

7. Bake in the preheated oven for about 15-20 minutes, or until the cheese is melted and bubbly.

8. Remove from the oven and sprinkle the chopped basil leaves over the mushrooms.

9. Drizzle balsamic glaze over the top for added flavor.

10. Serve the Caprese Stuffed Portobello Mushrooms warm as a delicious appetizer or side dish.

Spinach and Feta Omelette:

Ingredients:

- 3 large eggs

- 1/4 cup fresh spinach, chopped

- 1/4 cup feta cheese, crumbled

- 1 tablespoon olive oil

- Salt and pepper, to taste

Instructions:

1. Crack the eggs into a bowl and whisk them until well beaten. Season with salt and pepper.

2. Heat the olive oil in a non-stick skillet over medium heat.

3. Add the chopped spinach to the skillet and sauté for about 1-2 minutes, until wilted.

4. Pour the beaten eggs into the skillet, making sure they cover the entire bottom.

5. Cook the omelette for about 2-3 minutes, or until the edges start to set.

6. Sprinkle the crumbled feta cheese evenly over one half of the omelette.

7. Using a spatula, carefully fold the other half of the omelette over the cheese side.

8. Cook for another 1-2 minutes, or until the cheese is melted and the omelette is cooked through.

9. Slide the omelette onto a plate and serve hot.

Asian-Inspired Quinoa Bowl.

Ingredients:

- 1 cup quinoa

- 2 cups water

- 1 tablespoon sesame oil

- 2 cloves garlic, minced

- 1 tablespoon ginger, grated

- 1 cup mixed vegetables (such as carrots, bell peppers, broccoli, snap peas)

- 1 cup cooked protein (such as tofu, chicken, shrimp)

- 2 tablespoons soy sauce

- 1 tablespoon rice vinegar

- 1 tablespoon honey or maple syrup

- 1 tablespoon sesame seeds (optional)

- Green onions, chopped (for garnish)

Instructions:

1. Rinse the quinoa under cold water to remove any bitterness. In a saucepan, combine the rinsed quinoa and water. Bring to a boil, then reduce heat to low, cover, and simmer for about 15-20 minutes or until the quinoa is cooked and the water is absorbed. Fluff with a fork and set aside.

2. In a large skillet or wok, heat the sesame oil over medium heat. Add the minced garlic and grated ginger, and sauté for about 1-2 minutes until fragrant.

3. Add the mixed vegetables to the skillet and stir-fry for about 5-7 minutes until they are tender-crisp.

4. Push the vegetables to one side of the skillet and add the cooked protein to the other side. Cook for a few minutes until heated through.

5. In a small bowl, whisk together the soy sauce, rice vinegar, and honey/maple syrup. Pour the sauce over the vegetables and protein in the skillet. Stir everything together to coat evenly.

6. Add the cooked quinoa to the skillet and toss everything together until well combined and heated through.

7. Remove from heat and sprinkle with sesame seeds (if using) and chopped green onions for garnish.

8. Serve the Asian-Inspired Quinoa Bowl hot and enjoy!

Greek Chicken Pita Wrap:

Ingredients:

- 2 boneless, skinless chicken breasts

- 1 tablespoon olive oil

- 1 tablespoon lemon juice

- 1 teaspoon dried oregano

- Salt and pepper to taste

- 4 pita breads

- Tzatziki sauce

- Sliced tomatoes

- Sliced cucumbers

- Sliced red onions

- Crumbled feta cheese

- Fresh parsley (optional, for garnish)

Instructions:

1. In a bowl, combine olive oil, lemon juice, dried oregano, salt, and pepper. Mix well.

2. Add the chicken breasts to the bowl and coat them with the marinade. Let them marinate for at least 30 minutes, or overnight in the refrigerator for more flavor.

3. Preheat your grill or grill pan over medium-high heat.

4. Grill the chicken breasts for about 6-8 minutes per side, or until cooked through and no longer pink in the center. Remove from heat and let them rest for a few minutes.

5. Slice the grilled chicken into thin strips.

6. Warm the pita breads in a toaster or on a grill pan for a few seconds on each side.

7. Spread a generous amount of tzatziki sauce on each pita bread.

8. Place a few slices of grilled chicken on top of the tzatziki sauce.

9. Add sliced tomatoes, cucumbers, and red onions on top of the chicken.

10. Sprinkle crumbled feta cheese over the vegetables.

11. Garnish with fresh parsley, if desired.

12. Fold the pita breads in half and serve immediately.

Mediterranean Quinoa Salad:

Ingredients:

- 1 cup quinoa

- 2 cups water or vegetable broth

- 1 cup cherry tomatoes, halved

- 1 cucumber, diced

- 1/2 red onion, thinly sliced

- 1/2 cup Kalamata olives, pitted and halved

- 1/2 cup crumbled feta cheese

- 1/4 cup chopped fresh parsley

- 1/4 cup chopped fresh mint

- Juice of 1 lemon

- 3 tablespoons extra virgin olive oil

- Salt and pepper to taste

Instructions:

1. Rinse the quinoa under cold water to remove any bitterness.

2. In a saucepan, bring the water or vegetable broth to a boil. Add the quinoa and reduce the

heat to low. Cover and simmer for about 15-20 minutes, or until the quinoa is cooked and the liquid is absorbed. Remove from heat and let it cool.

3. In a large bowl, combine the cooked quinoa, cherry tomatoes, cucumber, red onion, Kalamata olives, feta cheese, parsley, and mint.

4. In a small bowl, whisk together the lemon juice, olive oil, salt, and pepper.

5. Pour the dressing over the quinoa salad and toss to combine.

6. Taste and adjust the seasoning if needed.

7. Let the salad sit for at least 15 minutes to allow the flavors to meld together.

8. Serve chilled or at room temperature.

Vegetarian Hummus Wrap.

Ingredients:

- Tortilla wrap

- Hummus

- Assorted vegetables (such as lettuce, cucumber, bell peppers, carrots, etc.)

- Optional: Feta cheese, olives, or any other desired toppings

Instructions:

1. Start by preparing your vegetables. Wash and slice them into thin strips or julienne them, depending on your preference.

2. Lay the tortilla wrap flat on a clean surface.

3. Spread a generous amount of hummus evenly over the tortilla, leaving a small border around the edges.

4. Place your prepared vegetables on top of the hummus, arranging them in a single layer.

5. If desired, add any additional toppings like feta cheese or olives.

6. Carefully roll the tortilla, starting from one end and tucking in the sides as you go, until you have a tight wrap.

7. If you prefer, you can cut the wrap in half or into smaller portions for easier handling.

8. Serve immediately and enjoy your delicious Vegetarian Hummus Wrap!

Satisfying Dinners for the Days Leading Up to Surgery

As you approach the significant journey of a hysterectomy, the days leading up to the surgery become a crucial time to nourish your body with satisfying and comforting meals. These dinner ideas are crafted to provide a sense of culinary comfort, focusing on nutrition and flavors to ease your mind and prepare your body. Each recipe is designed with ingredients that contribute to pre-operative wellness and provide the sustenance needed for the upcoming surgery.

Here are several recipes meticulously crafted to strengthen your body and ready it for the upcoming hysterectomy procedure.

Grilled Lemon Herb Chicken.

Ingredients:

- Chicken breasts or chicken thighs

- Lemon juice (from fresh lemons or bottled)

- Olive oil

- Garlic cloves, minced

- Fresh herbs (such as rosemary, thyme, or parsley), chopped

- Salt and pepper, to taste

Instructions:

1. In a bowl, combine the lemon juice, olive oil, minced garlic, chopped herbs, salt, and pepper. Mix well to create a marinade.

2. Place the chicken breasts or thighs in a shallow dish or a resealable plastic bag.

3. Pour the marinade over the chicken, making sure it is evenly coated. You can use a spoon or your hands to massage the marinade into the chicken.

4. Cover the dish or seal the bag and refrigerate for at least 30 minutes, or up to 24 hours for maximum flavor.

5. Preheat your grill to medium-high heat.

6. Remove the chicken from the marinade, allowing any excess marinade to drip off.

7. Place the chicken on the grill and cook for about 6-8 minutes per side, or until the internal temperature reaches 165°F (74°C) for chicken breasts or 175°F (79°C) for chicken thighs.

8. Once cooked, remove the chicken from the grill and let it rest for a few minutes before serving.

9. Serve the Grilled Lemon Herb Chicken with your choice of sides, such as roasted vegetables, salad, or rice.

Baked Salmon with Dill:

Ingredients:

- 1 pound of salmon fillets

- 2 tablespoons of olive oil

- 2 tablespoons of fresh dill, chopped

- 1 lemon, sliced

- Salt and pepper to taste

Instructions:

1. Preheat your oven to 375°F (190°C).

2. Place the salmon fillets on a baking sheet lined with parchment paper or aluminum foil.

3. Drizzle the olive oil over the salmon fillets, making sure to coat them evenly.

4. Sprinkle the chopped dill over the salmon, followed by salt and pepper to taste.

5. Place the lemon slices on top of the salmon fillets.

6. Fold the parchment paper or aluminum foil over the salmon, creating a packet to seal in the flavors.

7. Bake the salmon in the preheated oven for about 15-20 minutes, or until it is cooked through and flakes easily with a fork.

8. Once cooked, carefully open the packet and transfer the salmon to a serving dish.

9. Serve the baked salmon with dill hot and enjoy!

Quinoa and Roasted Vegetable Bowl:

Ingredients:

- 1 cup of quinoa

- 2 cups of water or vegetable broth

- 1 bell pepper, sliced

- 1 zucchini, sliced

- 1 red onion, sliced

- 1 cup of cherry tomatoes

- 2 tablespoons of olive oil

- 1 teaspoon of dried herbs (such as thyme, rosemary, or oregano)

- Salt and pepper to taste

- Optional toppings: avocado, feta cheese, or fresh herbs

Instructions:

1. Preheat your oven to 400°F (200°C).

2. Rinse the quinoa under cold water to remove any bitterness.

3. In a saucepan, bring the water or vegetable broth to a boil. Add the quinoa and reduce the heat to low. Cover and simmer for about 15-20 minutes, or until the quinoa is cooked and the liquid is absorbed. Fluff the quinoa with a fork and set aside.

4. In a large bowl, toss the sliced bell pepper, zucchini, red onion, and cherry tomatoes with olive oil, dried herbs, salt, and pepper.

5. Spread the vegetables in a single layer on a baking sheet lined with parchment paper or aluminum foil.

6. Roast the vegetables in the preheated oven for about 20-25 minutes, or until they are tender and slightly caramelized.

7. In serving bowls, layer the cooked quinoa and roasted vegetables.

8. Top with optional toppings such as avocado, feta cheese, or fresh herbs.

9. Serve the quinoa and roasted vegetable bowl warm and enjoy!

Lemon Garlic Shrimp Stir-Fry:

Ingredients:

- 1 pound of shrimp, peeled and deveined

- 2 tablespoons of olive oil

- 4 cloves of garlic, minced

- 1 teaspoon of grated lemon zest

- 2 tablespoons of lemon juice

- 1 tablespoon of soy sauce

- 1 tablespoon of honey

- 1 red bell pepper, sliced

- 1 yellow bell pepper, sliced

- 1 cup of snap peas

- Salt and pepper to taste

- Cooked rice or noodles for serving

Instructions:

1. In a small bowl, whisk together the minced garlic, lemon zest, lemon juice, soy sauce, and honey. Set aside.

2. Heat the olive oil in a large skillet or wok over medium-high heat.

3. Add the shrimp to the skillet and season with salt and pepper. Cook for 2-3 minutes until the shrimp turns pink and opaque. Remove the shrimp from the skillet and set aside.

4. In the same skillet, add the sliced bell peppers and snap peas. Stir-fry for about 3-4 minutes until the vegetables are crisp-tender.

5. Return the cooked shrimp to the skillet and pour the lemon garlic sauce over the shrimp and vegetables. Stir everything together to coat evenly.

6. Cook for an additional 1-2 minutes until the sauce thickens slightly.

7. Serve the Lemon Garlic Shrimp Stir-Fry over cooked rice or noodles.

Sweet Potato and Chickpea Curry:

Ingredients:

- 2 tablespoons of olive oil

- 1 onion, diced

- 3 cloves of garlic, minced

- 1 tablespoon of grated ginger

- 2 sweet potatoes, peeled and diced

- 1 can of chickpeas, drained and rinsed

- 1 can of coconut milk

- 1 can of diced tomatoes

- 2 tablespoons of curry powder

- 1 teaspoon of ground cumin

- 1 teaspoon of ground coriander

- 1/2 teaspoon of turmeric

- Salt and pepper to taste

- Fresh cilantro for garnish

- Cooked rice or naan bread for serving

Instructions:

1. Heat the olive oil in a large pot or skillet over medium heat.

2. Add the diced onion and cook until it becomes translucent, about 5 minutes.

3. Add the minced garlic and grated ginger to the pot and cook for an additional minute until fragrant.

4. Add the diced sweet potatoes, drained chickpeas, coconut milk, diced tomatoes, curry powder, ground cumin, ground coriander, turmeric, salt, and pepper to the pot. Stir everything together.

5. Bring the mixture to a boil, then reduce the heat to low and let it simmer for about 20-25 minutes until the sweet potatoes are tender.

6. Taste and adjust the seasoning if needed.

7. Serve the Sweet Potato and Chickpea Curry over cooked rice or with naan bread.

8. Garnish with fresh cilantro.

Turkey and Vegetable Skewers.

Ingredients:

- 1 pound of turkey breast, cut into cubes

- Assorted vegetables of your choice (such as bell peppers, zucchini, cherry tomatoes, red onions, mushrooms)

- Olive oil

- Salt and pepper to taste

- Optional marinade or seasoning of your choice (such as lemon juice, garlic, herbs, or spices)

Instructions:

1. If you're using wooden skewers, soak them in water for about 30 minutes to prevent them from burning on the grill.

2. Preheat your grill to medium-high heat.

3. In a large bowl, combine the turkey cubes with olive oil, salt, pepper, and any optional marinade or seasoning you prefer. Toss well to coat the turkey evenly.

4. Thread the turkey cubes onto the skewers, alternating with the assorted vegetables.

5. Brush the skewers with a little more olive oil to prevent sticking on the grill.

6. Place the skewers on the preheated grill and cook for about 10-12 minutes, turning occasionally, until the turkey is cooked through and the vegetables are tender.

7. Remove the skewers from the grill and let them rest for a few minutes before serving.

Spinach and Feta Stuffed Chicken Breast.

Ingredients:

- 2 boneless, skinless chicken breasts

- 2 cups of fresh spinach, chopped

- 1/2 cup of crumbled feta cheese

- 2 cloves of garlic, minced

- Salt and pepper to taste

- Olive oil

Instructions:

1. Preheat your oven to 375°F (190°C).

2. Butterfly the chicken breasts by slicing them horizontally, but not all the way through, so that you can open them like a book.

3. In a small bowl, mix together the chopped spinach, crumbled feta cheese, minced garlic, salt, and pepper.

4. Open the chicken breasts and evenly divide the spinach and feta mixture between them, spreading it over one side of each breast.

5. Fold the other side of the chicken breast over the filling, pressing gently to seal.

6. Heat a large oven-safe skillet over medium-high heat and add a drizzle of olive oil.

7. Place the stuffed chicken breasts in the skillet and cook for about 3-4 minutes on each side, until they are browned.

8. Transfer the skillet to the preheated oven and bake for about 20-25 minutes, or until the chicken is cooked through and no longer pink in the center.

9. Remove the skillet from the oven and let the chicken rest for a few minutes before serving.

Butternut Squash and Sage Risotto.

Ingredients:

- 1 small butternut squash, peeled, seeded, and diced into small cubes

- 1 cup Arborio rice

- 4 cups vegetable or chicken broth

- 1 small onion, finely chopped

- 2 cloves of garlic, minced

- 1/4 cup white wine (optional)

- 2 tablespoons olive oil

- 2 tablespoons butter

- 1/4 cup grated Parmesan cheese

- Fresh sage leaves, chopped

- Salt and pepper to taste

Instructions:

1. In a large saucepan, heat the olive oil and butter over medium heat. Add the chopped onion and minced garlic, and sauté until they become translucent.

2. Add the Arborio rice to the saucepan and stir it for a couple of minutes until it becomes slightly toasted.

3. If using white wine, pour it into the saucepan and stir until it evaporates.

4. Begin adding the vegetable or chicken broth to the saucepan, one ladle at a time, stirring continuously. Allow the rice to absorb the broth before adding more. Repeat this process until the rice is cooked al dente, which usually takes about 20-25 minutes.

5. While the risotto is cooking, in a separate pan, heat some olive oil and sauté the diced butternut squash until it becomes tender and slightly caramelized. Season with salt and pepper.

6. Once the risotto is cooked, add the sautéed butternut squash, grated Parmesan cheese, and chopped sage leaves. Stir well to combine all the ingredients.

7. Taste and adjust the seasoning with salt and pepper if needed.

8. Serve the Butternut Squash and Sage Risotto hot, garnished with some additional grated Parmesan cheese and sage leaves if desired.

Ginger Lime Tofu Stir-Fry.

Ingredients:

- 1 block of firm tofu, drained and pressed

- 2 tablespoons of soy sauce

- 2 tablespoons of lime juice

- 1 tablespoon of ginger, grated

- 2 cloves of garlic, minced

- 1 tablespoon of sesame oil

- 1 tablespoon of vegetable oil

- 1 bell pepper, sliced

- 1 carrot, julienned

- 1 cup of broccoli florets

- 1 cup of snap peas

- Salt and pepper to taste

- Cooked rice or noodles for serving

Instructions:

1. Start by preparing the tofu. Cut the tofu into cubes or slices, whichever you prefer. In a bowl, combine soy sauce, lime juice, grated ginger, and minced garlic. Add the tofu to the bowl and let it marinate for at least 15 minutes.

2. Heat the sesame oil and vegetable oil in a large skillet or wok over medium-high heat. Once the oil is hot, add the marinated tofu (reserving the marinade) and cook until golden brown on all sides. Remove the tofu from the skillet and set it aside.

3. In the same skillet, add the bell pepper, carrot, broccoli, and snap peas. Stir-fry the vegetables for about 5-7 minutes until they are tender-crisp.

4. While the vegetables are cooking, pour the reserved marinade into a small saucepan and bring it to a simmer. Let it cook for a few minutes until it thickens slightly.

5. Once the vegetables are cooked, add the tofu back to the skillet and pour the thickened marinade over everything. Stir well to coat the tofu and vegetables evenly. Cook for an additional 2-3 minutes to heat everything through.

6. Season with salt and pepper to taste. Serve the Ginger-Lime Tofu Stir-Fry over cooked rice or noodles.

Caprese Salad with Grilled Chicken:

Ingredients:

- 2 boneless, skinless chicken breasts

- 2 tablespoons olive oil

- Salt and pepper, to taste

- 2 large tomatoes

- 8 ounces fresh mozzarella cheese

- Fresh basil leaves

- Balsamic glaze

- Salt and pepper, to taste

Instructions:

1. Preheat your grill to medium-high heat.

2. Season the chicken breasts with salt, pepper, and olive oil.

3. Grill the chicken for about 6-8 minutes per side, or until cooked through. Make sure the internal temperature reaches 165°F (74°C).

4. While the chicken is grilling, slice the tomatoes and mozzarella cheese into thick slices.

5. Arrange the tomato and mozzarella slices on a serving platter, alternating between them.

6. Once the chicken is cooked, let it rest for a few minutes, then slice it into thin strips.

7. Place the grilled chicken strips on top of the tomato and mozzarella slices.

8. Garnish with fresh basil leaves.

9. Drizzle balsamic glaze over the salad.

10. Season with salt and pepper to taste.

11. Serve immediately and enjoy!

Hydrating and Healing Beverages

As you embark on the path toward a hysterectomy, the significance of hydration cannot be overstated. Fluids play a crucial role in maintaining optimal bodily functions, aiding in digestion, and promoting overall well-being.

Cucumber-Mint Infused Water:

Ingredients:

- 1 cucumber

- 10-12 fresh mint leaves

- Water

Instructions:

1. Wash the cucumber thoroughly and slice it into thin rounds.

2. Rinse the mint leaves under cold water to remove any dirt or debris.

3. In a pitcher or large jar, add the cucumber slices and mint leaves.

4. Fill the pitcher or jar with water, covering the cucumber and mint completely.

5. Stir gently to release the flavors.

6. Cover the pitcher or jar and refrigerate for at least 2 hours, or overnight for a stronger flavor.

7. When ready to serve, you can strain the infused water to remove the cucumber and mint leaves, or leave them in for added visual appeal.

8. Pour the infused water into glasses filled with ice cubes.

9. Enjoy the refreshing cucumber-mint infused water!

Berry-Mint Smoothie.

Ingredients:

- 1 cup of mixed berries (such as strawberries, blueberries, raspberries)

- 1 ripe banana

- 1 cup of spinach or kale (optional)

- 1/2 cup of plain or Greek yogurt

- 1/2 cup of milk (dairy or plant-based)

- 1 tablespoon of honey or maple syrup (optional, for sweetness)

- A handful of fresh mint leaves

- Ice cubes (optional, for a colder smoothie)

Instructions:

1. Wash the berries and remove any stems or leaves.

2. Peel the banana and break it into smaller chunks.

3. If using spinach or kale, wash and remove any tough stems.

4. Place the berries, banana, spinach or kale (if using), yogurt, milk, honey or maple syrup (if using), and mint leaves into a blender.

5. Blend on high speed until all the ingredients are well combined and smooth.

6. If desired, add a few ice cubes and blend again until the smoothie reaches your desired consistency.

7. Taste the smoothie and adjust the sweetness or mint flavor if needed by adding more honey, maple syrup, or mint leaves.

8. Pour the smoothie into glasses and serve immediately.

Ginger-Turmeric Tea.

Ingredients:

- 1 inch piece of fresh ginger, peeled and thinly sliced

- 1 teaspoon of ground turmeric

- 2 cups of water

- 1 tablespoon of honey or maple syrup (optional, for sweetness)

- Juice of half a lemon (optional, for added flavor)

Instructions:

1. In a small saucepan, bring the water to a boil.

2. Add the sliced ginger and ground turmeric to the boiling water.

3. Reduce the heat to low and let the mixture simmer for about 10 minutes.

4. After 10 minutes, remove the saucepan from the heat and let the tea steep for an additional 5 minutes.

5. Strain the tea to remove the ginger and turmeric pieces.

6. If desired, add honey or maple syrup to sweeten the tea, and lemon juice for added flavor.

7. Stir well to combine the sweetener and lemon juice.

8. Pour the tea into cups and serve hot.

Coconut Water Refresher recipe.

Ingredients:

- 1 cup of coconut water

- 1/2 cup of pineapple juice

- 1/4 cup of lime juice

- 2 tablespoons of honey or sweetener of your choice

- Ice cubes

- Optional: mint leaves or pineapple slices for garnish

Instructions:

1. In a pitcher or large glass, combine the coconut water, pineapple juice, lime juice, and honey. Stir well until the honey is fully dissolved.

2. Taste the mixture and adjust the sweetness or tartness according to your preference by adding more honey or lime juice if needed.

3. Fill serving glasses with ice cubes.

4. Pour the coconut water mixture over the ice cubes, dividing it evenly among the glasses.

5. Garnish with mint leaves or pineapple slices if desired.

6. Stir gently to combine the flavors.

7. Serve immediately and enjoy your refreshing Coconut Water Refresher!

Chamomile-Lavender Infusion recipe.

Ingredients:

- 2 cups of water

- 2 chamomile tea bags or 2 tablespoons of loose chamomile flowers

- 1 tablespoon of dried lavender flowers or 2 lavender tea bags

- Honey or sweetener of your choice (optional)

Instructions:

1. In a small saucepan, bring the water to a boil.

2. Once the water is boiling, remove it from the heat and add the chamomile tea bags or loose chamomile flowers and dried lavender flowers or lavender tea bags.

3. Cover the saucepan with a lid and let the mixture steep for about 5-10 minutes, or until the desired strength is reached.

4. Remove the tea bags or strain out the loose flowers using a fine-mesh strainer.

5. If desired, add honey or sweetener to taste and stir until dissolved.

6. Pour the infusion into cups or mugs and serve hot.

7. You can also let the infusion cool down and serve it over ice for a refreshing iced version.

I hope you find this helpful! Let me know if you have any more questions.

CHAPTER 3

Importance of post-operative nutrition

The importance of post-operative nutrition cannot be overstated. After a hysterectomy, the body goes through a healing process that requires proper nourishment. Adequate nutrition can help to promote wound healing, reduce inflammation, boost the immune system, and provide the energy needed for recovery.

Soft and Easy-to-Digest Foods

Navigating the days leading up to a hysterectomy calls for a thoughtful approach to your diet. These gentle dishes aim to ease digestion while ensuring you receive essential nutrients to support your well-being.

Creamy Butternut Squash Soup.

Ingredients:

- 1 medium-sized butternut squash

- 1 tablespoon olive oil

- 1 medium-sized onion, chopped

- 2 cloves of garlic, minced

- 4 cups vegetable or chicken broth

- 1 teaspoon dried thyme

- 1/2 teaspoon ground nutmeg

- Salt and pepper to taste

- 1/2 cup heavy cream (optional)

Instructions:

1. Start by preparing the butternut squash. Cut it in half lengthwise and scoop out the seeds and fibers. Peel the skin off using a vegetable peeler or a knife, then chop the squash into small cubes.

2. Heat the olive oil in a large pot over medium heat. Add the chopped onion and minced garlic, and sauté until they become translucent and fragrant.

3. Add the cubed butternut squash to the pot and stir well to combine with the onions and garlic. Cook for about 5 minutes, stirring occasionally.

4. Pour in the vegetable or chicken broth, making sure it covers the squash. Add the dried thyme, ground nutmeg, salt, and pepper. Stir everything together.

5. Bring the mixture to a boil, then reduce the heat to low and let it simmer for about 20-25 minutes, or until the butternut squash is tender and easily mashed with a fork.

6. Once the squash is cooked, use an immersion blender or transfer the mixture to a blender or

food processor to puree until smooth. Be careful when blending hot liquids.

7. If desired, stir in the heavy cream to make the soup extra creamy. Adjust the seasoning with salt and pepper to taste.

8. Return the pot to the stove and heat the soup over low heat until warmed through.

9. Serve the creamy butternut squash soup hot, garnished with a sprinkle of nutmeg or a drizzle of cream, if desired.

Mashed Cauliflower with Garlic and Herbs.
Ingredients:

- 1 large head of cauliflower

- 2 cloves of garlic, minced

- 2 tablespoons of olive oil

- 1/4 cup of vegetable broth (or chicken broth)

- 1/4 cup of grated Parmesan cheese (optional)

- 1 tablespoon of chopped fresh herbs (such as parsley, thyme, or rosemary)

- Salt and pepper to taste

Instructions:

1. Start by cutting the cauliflower into florets, discarding the tough stem. Rinse the florets under cold water and drain well.

2. In a large pot, bring water to a boil and add a pinch of salt. Add the cauliflower florets and

cook for about 10-12 minutes, or until they are tender when pierced with a fork.

3. While the cauliflower is cooking, heat the olive oil in a small skillet over medium heat. Add the minced garlic and sauté for about 1-2 minutes, until fragrant. Be careful not to burn the garlic.

4. Once the cauliflower is cooked, drain it well and transfer it to a large mixing bowl. Use a potato masher or a fork to mash the cauliflower until it reaches your desired consistency.

5. Add the sautéed garlic, vegetable broth, grated Parmesan cheese (if using), and chopped fresh herbs to the mashed cauliflower. Mix well to combine.

6. Season with salt and pepper to taste. Adjust the seasoning as needed.

7. Serve the mashed cauliflower with garlic and herbs warm as a side dish or as a healthier alternative to mashed potatoes.

I hope you enjoy making and eating this delicious mashed cauliflower recipe! Let me know if you have any more questions.

Banana Oat Pancakes.

Ingredients:

- 1 ripe banana

- 1 cup of rolled oats

- 1/2 cup of milk (dairy or plant-based)

- 1 teaspoon of baking powder

- 1/2 teaspoon of cinnamon (optional)

- 1/2 teaspoon of vanilla extract (optional)

- 1 tablespoon of honey or maple syrup (optional)

- Pinch of salt

- Cooking oil or butter for greasing the pan

Instructions:

1. In a blender or food processor, add the ripe banana, rolled oats, milk, baking powder, cinnamon (if using), vanilla extract (if using), honey or maple syrup (if using), and a pinch of salt.

2. Blend or process the ingredients until you have a smooth batter. If the batter is too thick, you can add a little more milk to thin it out.

3. Heat a non-stick skillet or griddle over medium heat. Grease the surface with cooking oil or butter.

4. Pour about 1/4 cup of the pancake batter onto the skillet for each pancake. You can make them smaller or larger depending on your preference.

5. Cook the pancakes for about 2-3 minutes, or until bubbles start to form on the surface. Flip the pancakes and cook for an additional 1-2 minutes, or until they are golden brown and cooked through.

6. Repeat the process with the remaining batter, adding more oil or butter to the skillet as needed.

7. Serve the banana oat pancakes warm with your favorite toppings, such as fresh fruit, yogurt, honey, or maple syrup.

Ginger Carrot Puree.

Ingredients:

- 1 pound of carrots, peeled and chopped

- 1 tablespoon of fresh ginger, grated

- 2 cloves of garlic, minced

- 1 tablespoon of olive oil

- 1 cup of vegetable broth

- Salt and pepper to taste

Instructions:

1. In a large pot, heat the olive oil over medium heat.

2. Add the minced garlic and grated ginger to the pot and sauté for about 1 minute until fragrant.

3. Add the chopped carrots to the pot and stir to coat them with the ginger and garlic mixture.

4. Pour in the vegetable broth and bring it to a boil.

5. Reduce the heat to low, cover the pot, and let the carrots simmer for about 15-20 minutes until they are tender.

6. Once the carrots are cooked, remove the pot from the heat and let it cool slightly.

7. Using a blender or food processor, puree the cooked carrots until smooth and creamy.

8. If the puree is too thick, you can add a little more vegetable broth or water to achieve your desired consistency.

9. Season the ginger carrot puree with salt and pepper to taste.

10. Serve the puree warm as a side dish or use it as a base for other recipes.

Applesauce Chia Pudding.

Ingredients:

- 1 cup of unsweetened applesauce

- 1 cup of almond milk (or any other milk of your choice)

- 1/4 cup of chia seeds

- 1 tablespoon of honey or maple syrup (optional)

- 1/2 teaspoon of vanilla extract

- 1/2 teaspoon of ground cinnamon (optional)

- Toppings of your choice (e.g., fresh fruits, nuts, granola)

Instructions:

1. In a bowl, combine the unsweetened applesauce, almond milk, chia seeds, honey or maple syrup (if using), vanilla extract, and

ground cinnamon (if using). Stir well to combine all the ingredients.

2. Let the mixture sit for about 5 minutes, then give it another stir to prevent the chia seeds from clumping together.

3. Cover the bowl and refrigerate it for at least 2 hours or overnight to allow the chia seeds to absorb the liquid and thicken the pudding.

4. After the pudding has set, give it a good stir to break up any clumps and evenly distribute the chia seeds.

5. If the pudding is too thick for your liking, you can add a little more almond milk to thin it out.

6. Serve the applesauce chia pudding in individual bowls or jars and top it with your

favorite toppings, such as fresh fruits, nuts, or granola.

7. Enjoy the pudding immediately or refrigerate it for later use.

Soft Scrambled Eggs with Spinach.

Ingredients:

- 4 large eggs

- 1 cup fresh spinach, chopped

- Salt and pepper to taste

- 1 tablespoon butter or oil (for cooking)

Instructions:

1. Crack the eggs into a bowl and whisk them until well beaten. Season with salt and pepper according to your taste.

2. Heat a non-stick skillet over medium heat and add the butter or oil. Allow it to melt and coat the bottom of the skillet.

3. Add the chopped spinach to the skillet and sauté for a couple of minutes until it wilts.

4. Pour the beaten eggs into the skillet with the spinach. Let the eggs cook undisturbed for a minute or two until the edges start to set.

5. Using a spatula, gently push the cooked edges towards the center, allowing the uncooked eggs to flow to the edges.

6. Continue this process of pushing and folding the eggs until they are mostly cooked but still slightly runny.

7. Remove the skillet from heat and let the residual heat finish cooking the eggs. They should be soft and slightly creamy.

8. Season with additional salt and pepper if needed.

9. Serve the soft scrambled eggs with spinach immediately while they are still warm.

Pumpkin Risotto.

Ingredients:

- 1 small pumpkin or butternut squash, peeled, seeded, and cut into small cubes

- 1 onion, finely chopped

- 2 cloves of garlic, minced

- 1 1/2 cups Arborio rice

- 4 cups vegetable or chicken broth

- 1/2 cup white wine (optional)

- 1/2 cup grated Parmesan cheese

- 2 tablespoons butter

- Salt and pepper to taste

- Fresh parsley or sage for garnish (optional)

Instructions:

1. In a large saucepan, heat some olive oil over medium heat. Add the chopped onion and minced garlic, and sauté until they become translucent.

2. Add the Arborio rice to the saucepan and stir it for a minute or two until it becomes slightly toasted.

3. If using, pour in the white wine and stir until it is absorbed by the rice.

4. Begin adding the vegetable or chicken broth to the saucepan, one ladle at a time. Stir the rice constantly and wait for the broth to be absorbed before adding more.

5. After about 15-20 minutes, when the rice is almost cooked, add the pumpkin cubes to the saucepan. Continue adding the broth and stirring until the rice and pumpkin are fully cooked and creamy.

6. Stir in the grated Parmesan cheese and butter until they melt and incorporate into the risotto.

7. Season with salt and pepper to taste.

8. Remove the saucepan from heat and let the risotto rest for a few minutes.

9. Serve the Pumpkin Risotto hot, garnished with fresh parsley or sage if desired.

Yogurt and Berry Smoothie Bowl.

Ingredients:

- 1 cup of yogurt (you can use any flavor you prefer)

- 1 cup of frozen berries (such as strawberries, blueberries, or raspberries)

- 1 ripe banana

- 1/4 cup of milk (you can use any type of milk, such as dairy milk or plant-based milk)

- Toppings of your choice (such as granola, sliced fruits, nuts, or seeds)

Instructions:

1. In a blender, add the yogurt, frozen berries, ripe banana, and milk.

2. Blend the ingredients until smooth and well combined. If the mixture is too thick, you can add a little more milk to achieve your desired consistency.

3. Once the smoothie is ready, pour it into a bowl.

4. Now it's time to add your favorite toppings! You can sprinkle some granola, sliced fruits, nuts, or seeds on top of the smoothie bowl.

5. Enjoy your delicious Yogurt and Berry Smoothie Bowl!

Silken Tofu Chocolate Pudding:

Ingredients:

- 1 package (12-14 ounces) of silken tofu

- 1/4 cup of cocoa powder

- 1/4 cup of sweetener (such as maple syrup, agave nectar, or honey)

- 1 teaspoon of vanilla extract

- Optional toppings (such as whipped cream, chocolate shavings, or fresh berries)

Instructions:

1. Drain the silken tofu and pat it dry with a paper towel.

2. In a blender or food processor, add the silken tofu, cocoa powder, sweetener, and vanilla extract.

3. Blend the ingredients until smooth and creamy. You may need to scrape down the sides of the blender or food processor a few times to ensure everything is well mixed.

4. Taste the pudding and adjust the sweetness or cocoa flavor to your liking by adding more sweetener or cocoa powder if desired.

5. Once the pudding is smooth and well combined, transfer it to serving dishes or bowls.

6. Refrigerate the pudding for at least 1-2 hours to allow it to set and chill.

7. Before serving, you can add optional toppings such as whipped cream, chocolate shavings, or fresh berries.

8. Enjoy your Silken Tofu Chocolate Pudding!

Foods to Aid in Wound Healing

In the lead-up to a significant surgical procedure like a hysterectomy, the importance of nourishing your body with foods that support wound healing cannot be overstated. These dishes are crafted to fortify your body, enhance resilience, and lay the foundation for a smoother recovery process. Here are some general tips for post-operative nutrition that may aid in wound healing:

1. Protein-rich foods: Consuming adequate amounts of protein is essential for wound healing. Good sources of protein include lean meats, poultry, fish, eggs, dairy products, legumes, and tofu.

2. Vitamin C: This vitamin plays a crucial role in collagen synthesis, which is important for wound healing. Foods rich in vitamin C include citrus fruits, strawberries, kiwi, bell peppers, broccoli, and tomatoes.

3. Zinc: Zinc is involved in various aspects of wound healing, including cell growth and immune function. Foods high in zinc include oysters, beef, poultry, beans, nuts, and whole grains.

4. Omega-3 fatty acids: These healthy fats have anti-inflammatory properties and may help with wound healing. Good sources of omega-3 fatty

acids include fatty fish (such as salmon and mackerel), walnuts, flaxseeds, and chia seeds.

5. Fiber: Adequate fiber intake can help maintain regular bowel movements, which is important after surgery. Whole grains, fruits, vegetables, and legumes are good sources of fiber.

CHAPTER 4

Post-Operative Recipe Collection

In the aftermath of a hysterectomy, a nourishing diet takes center stage in supporting recovery. This post-operative recipe collection is crafted with the understanding that comfort and nutrition are integral to the healing process. These comforting soups and broths are not just delicious; they are tailored to provide essential nutrients, promote hydration, and bring a sense of warmth to your post-surgery days.

Comforting Soups and Broths

As you embark on your post-hysterectomy journey, the healing power of comforting soups and broths becomes an integral part of your recovery. These recipes are thoughtfully crafted to bring both warmth and nutritional benefits to your post-operative days.

Healing chicken noodle soup recipe.

Ingredients:

- 1 whole chicken, cut into pieces

- 8 cups of chicken broth

- 1 onion, diced

- 3 carrots, sliced

- 3 celery stalks, sliced

- 2 cloves of garlic, minced

- 1 teaspoon of dried thyme

- 1 bay leaf

- Salt and pepper to taste

- 8 ounces of egg noodles

- Fresh parsley, chopped (for garnish)

Instructions:

1. In a large pot, bring the chicken broth to a boil. Add the chicken pieces and simmer for about 30 minutes, or until the chicken is cooked through. Remove the chicken from the pot and set it aside to cool.

2. In the same pot, add the diced onion, sliced carrots, sliced celery, minced garlic, dried thyme,

and bay leaf. Season with salt and pepper to taste. Simmer for about 15-20 minutes, or until the vegetables are tender.

3. While the vegetables are cooking, shred the cooked chicken into bite-sized pieces, discarding the skin and bones.

4. Once the vegetables are tender, add the shredded chicken back into the pot. Stir in the egg noodles and cook according to the package instructions, usually about 8-10 minutes.

5. Remove the bay leaf from the pot. Taste and adjust the seasoning if needed.

6. Serve the healing chicken noodle soup hot, garnished with fresh chopped parsley.

NB: Please note that this recipe is a general suggestion and may need to be modified based on your specific dietary needs and preferences. It is always a good idea to consult with your healthcare provider or a registered dietitian for personalized advice.

Ginger Turmeric Broth.

Ingredients:

- 2 cups vegetable broth

- 1 cup water

- 1-inch piece of fresh ginger, peeled and sliced

- 1 teaspoon ground turmeric

- 1 tablespoon soy sauce or tamari (optional)

- 1 tablespoon maple syrup or honey (optional)

- Salt and pepper to taste

Instructions:

1. In a medium-sized pot, combine the vegetable broth and water.

2. Add the sliced ginger and ground turmeric to the pot.

3. Bring the mixture to a boil over medium heat.

4. Once it reaches a boil, reduce the heat to low and let it simmer for about 15-20 minutes to allow the flavors to infuse.

5. If desired, you can add soy sauce or tamari for extra flavor and maple syrup or honey for a touch

of sweetness. Adjust the amounts according to your taste preferences.

6. Season with salt and pepper to taste.

7. Remove the pot from the heat and strain the broth to remove the ginger slices.

8. Your Ginger Turmeric Broth is now ready to be used in your favorite recipes or enjoyed on its own as a nourishing drink.

Lentil and Kale Soup.

Ingredients:

- 1 cup dried lentils, rinsed and drained

- 1 tablespoon olive oil

- 1 onion, diced

- 2 carrots, diced

- 2 celery stalks, diced

- 3 cloves garlic, minced

- 4 cups vegetable broth

- 2 cups water

- 1 can diced tomatoes (14.5 ounces)

- 2 cups chopped kale

- 1 teaspoon dried thyme

- 1 teaspoon dried oregano

- Salt and pepper to taste

Instructions:

1. Heat the olive oil in a large pot over medium heat.

2. Add the diced onion, carrots, and celery to the pot. Cook for about 5 minutes until the vegetables start to soften.

3. Add the minced garlic and cook for an additional minute.

4. Add the rinsed lentils, vegetable broth, water, diced tomatoes (with their juice), dried thyme, and dried oregano to the pot. Stir to combine.

5. Bring the mixture to a boil, then reduce the heat to low and let it simmer for about 20-25 minutes until the lentils are tender.

6. Stir in the chopped kale and cook for an additional 5 minutes until the kale wilts.

7. Season with salt and pepper to taste.

8. Remove the pot from the heat and let the soup cool slightly before serving.

Miso Mushroom Broth.

Ingredients:

- 4 cups vegetable broth

- 1 cup sliced mushrooms (any variety you prefer)

- 2 tablespoons miso paste

- 1 tablespoon soy sauce

- 1 tablespoon sesame oil

- 2 cloves garlic, minced

- 1-inch piece of ginger, grated

- 1 green onion, chopped (optional)

- Salt and pepper to taste

Instructions:

1. In a large pot, heat the sesame oil over medium heat.

2. Add the minced garlic and grated ginger to the pot and sauté for about 1-2 minutes until fragrant.

3. Add the sliced mushrooms to the pot and cook for another 3-4 minutes until they start to soften.

4. Pour in the vegetable broth and bring it to a boil. Reduce the heat and let it simmer for about 10 minutes to allow the flavors to meld together.

5. In a small bowl, whisk together the miso paste and soy sauce until well combined.

6. Add the miso-soy sauce mixture to the pot and stir well to incorporate it into the broth.

7. Let the broth simmer for an additional 5 minutes to ensure the miso paste is fully dissolved and incorporated.

8. Taste the broth and season with salt and pepper as desired.

9. Remove the pot from heat and serve the Miso Mushroom Broth hot.

10. Garnish with chopped green onions, if desired.

Roasted Tomato Basil Soup.

Ingredients:

- 2 pounds tomatoes, halved

- 1 onion, chopped

- 4 cloves garlic, minced

- 2 tablespoons olive oil

- 1 teaspoon dried basil

- 1/2 teaspoon dried oregano

- 4 cups vegetable broth

- 1/4 cup tomato paste

- 1/4 cup fresh basil leaves, chopped

- Salt and pepper to taste

Instructions:

1. Preheat your oven to 400°F (200°C).

2. Place the halved tomatoes, chopped onion, and minced garlic on a baking sheet. Drizzle with olive oil and sprinkle with dried basil, dried oregano, salt, and pepper.

3. Roast the tomato mixture in the preheated oven for about 30-40 minutes until the tomatoes are soft and slightly caramelized.

4. Transfer the roasted tomatoes, onions, and garlic to a large pot. Add the vegetable broth and tomato paste.

5. Bring the mixture to a boil, then reduce the heat and let it simmer for about 15-20 minutes to allow the flavors to meld together.

6. Use an immersion blender or transfer the soup to a blender to puree until smooth.

7. Return the soup to the pot and stir in the fresh basil leaves. Simmer for an additional 5 minutes.

8. Taste the soup and season with salt and pepper as desired.

9. Remove the pot from heat and serve the Roasted Tomato Basil Soup hot.

10. You can garnish with additional fresh basil leaves, if desired.

Spinach and Chickpea Stew.

Ingredients:

- 1 tablespoon olive oil

- 1 onion, diced

- 3 cloves of garlic, minced

- 1 teaspoon cumin

- 1 teaspoon paprika

- 1/2 teaspoon turmeric

- 1/4 teaspoon cayenne pepper (optional, for some heat)

- 1 can (14 ounces) diced tomatoes

- 2 cans (14 ounces each) chickpeas, drained and rinsed

- 4 cups vegetable broth

- 4 cups fresh spinach leaves

- Salt and pepper to taste

Instructions:

1. Heat the olive oil in a large pot over medium heat.

2. Add the diced onion and minced garlic to the pot and sauté until the onion becomes translucent and fragrant.

3. Stir in the cumin, paprika, turmeric, and cayenne pepper (if using) and cook for another minute to toast the spices.

4. Add the diced tomatoes (with their juices) to the pot and stir well.

5. Add the drained and rinsed chickpeas to the pot, followed by the vegetable broth. Stir everything together.

6. Bring the stew to a boil, then reduce the heat to low and let it simmer for about 15-20 minutes to allow the flavors to meld together.

7. Stir in the fresh spinach leaves and let them wilt in the stew for a few minutes.

8. Season with salt and pepper to taste.

9. Serve the Spinach and Chickpea Stew hot, and you can garnish it with some fresh herbs or a squeeze of lemon juice if desired.

Cauliflower and Leek Chowder.

Ingredients:

- 1 tablespoon olive oil

- 2 leeks, white and light green parts only, sliced

- 3 cloves of garlic, minced

- 1 head of cauliflower, chopped into florets

- 4 cups vegetable broth

- 1 cup milk (or plant-based milk for a vegan option)

- 1/2 teaspoon dried thyme

- Salt and pepper to taste

- Optional toppings: chopped chives, grated cheese, crumbled bacon

Instructions:

1. Heat the olive oil in a large pot over medium heat.

2. Add the sliced leeks and minced garlic to the pot and sauté until the leeks become soft and fragrant.

3. Add the chopped cauliflower florets to the pot and stir well.

4. Pour in the vegetable broth and bring the mixture to a boil.

5. Reduce the heat to low and let the chowder simmer for about 15-20 minutes, or until the cauliflower is tender.

6. Using an immersion blender or a regular blender, puree the soup until smooth and creamy.

7. Return the pot to the stove and stir in the milk and dried thyme.

8. Season with salt and pepper to taste.

9. Heat the chowder over low heat until warmed through.

10. Serve the Cauliflower and Leek Chowder hot, and you can garnish it with chopped chives, grated cheese, or crumbled bacon if desired.

Carrot Ginger Soup:

Ingredients:

- 1 pound carrots, peeled and chopped

- 1 onion, chopped

- 2 cloves garlic, minced

- 1 tablespoon fresh ginger, grated

- 4 cups vegetable broth

- 1 cup coconut milk

- 2 tablespoons olive oil

- Salt and pepper to taste

Instructions:

1. Heat the olive oil in a large pot over medium heat. Add the chopped onion and cook until it becomes translucent, about 5 minutes.

2. Add the minced garlic and grated ginger to the pot and cook for another 1-2 minutes, until fragrant.

3. Add the chopped carrots to the pot and stir to combine with the onion, garlic, and ginger.

4. Pour in the vegetable broth and bring the mixture to a boil. Reduce the heat to low, cover the pot, and simmer for about 20-25 minutes, or until the carrots are tender.

5. Use an immersion blender or transfer the soup to a blender to puree until smooth.

6. Return the pureed soup to the pot and stir in the coconut milk. Season with salt and pepper to taste.

7. Heat the soup over low heat until warmed through.

8. Serve hot and enjoy!

Soothing Lemon Dill Broth with Orzo:

Ingredients:

- 4 cups vegetable or chicken broth

- 1 cup orzo pasta

- 1 lemon, juiced

- 2 tablespoons fresh dill, chopped

- Salt and pepper to taste

Instructions:

1. In a large pot, bring the vegetable or chicken broth to a boil.

2. Add the orzo pasta to the boiling broth and cook according to the package instructions until al dente.

3. Once the orzo is cooked, reduce the heat to low and add the lemon juice and fresh dill to the pot.

4. Stir well to combine and let the flavors meld together for a few minutes.

5. Season with salt and pepper to taste.

6. Serve the soothing lemon dill broth with orzo hot and enjoy!

Gentle and Healing Smoothies

Smoothies are not just refreshing beverages; they can be soothing, nutrient-packed elixirs tailored to support your body's healing journey after a hysterectomy.

Tropical Turmeric Smoothie:

Ingredients:

- 1 cup frozen pineapple chunks

- 1 ripe banana

- 1 cup coconut milk (or any other milk of your choice)

- 1 teaspoon turmeric powder

- 1 tablespoon chia seeds

- 1 tablespoon honey or maple syrup (optional, for sweetness)

- Ice cubes (optional, for a colder smoothie)

Instructions:

1. In a blender, combine the frozen pineapple chunks, ripe banana, coconut milk, turmeric powder, chia seeds, and honey or maple syrup (if desired).

2. Blend on high speed until smooth and creamy.

3. If you prefer a colder smoothie, add a few ice cubes and blend again until well combined.

4. Pour the tropical turmeric smoothie into a glass and enjoy!

Pineapple Mint Cooler.

Ingredients:

- 2 cups pineapple chunks (fresh or canned)

- 1/4 cup fresh mint leaves

- 1/4 cup lime juice

- 2 tablespoons honey or sugar (adjust to taste)

- 2 cups sparkling water or club soda

- Ice cubes

Instructions:

1. In a blender, combine the pineapple chunks, fresh mint leaves, lime juice, and honey (or sugar).

2. Blend until smooth and well combined.

3. Strain the mixture through a fine-mesh sieve to remove any pulp or solids.

4. In a pitcher, combine the strained pineapple-mint mixture with sparkling water or club soda.

5. Stir well to combine.

6. Fill glasses with ice cubes and pour the Pineapple Mint Cooler over the ice.

7. Garnish with additional mint leaves or pineapple wedges, if desired.

8. Serve chilled and enjoy!

Banana Almond Dream.

Ingredients:

- 2 ripe bananas

- 1 cup almond milk

- 1 tablespoon almond butter

- 1 tablespoon honey or maple syrup (adjust to taste)

- 1/2 teaspoon vanilla extract

- Ice cubes

Instructions:

1. Peel the bananas and break them into chunks.

2. In a blender, combine the banana chunks, almond milk, almond butter, honey (or maple syrup), and vanilla extract.

3. Blend until smooth and creamy.

4. If desired, add a few ice cubes to make the drink colder and thicker.

5. Blend again until the ice cubes are fully incorporated.

6. Pour the Banana Almond Dream into glasses.

7. Serve chilled and enjoy!

Chamomile Honey Soothe

Chamomile Honey Soothe typically include chamomile flowers, honey, and water.

Instructions

1. Boil 1 cup of water in a small saucepan.

2. Once the water is boiling, remove it from heat and add 2 tablespoons of dried chamomile flowers.

3. Cover the saucepan and let the chamomile steep in the hot water for about 10 minutes.

4. After steeping, strain the chamomile flowers from the water using a fine-mesh strainer or cheesecloth.

5. Add 1-2 tablespoons of honey to the chamomile-infused water and stir until the honey is dissolved.

6. Let the mixture cool down to a comfortable temperature.

7. You can either drink the chamomile honey soothe as a warm tea or apply it topically to soothe skin irritations.

Mango Coconut Serenity

Mango Coconut Serenity includes mango, coconut milk, ice, and optionally, sweetener such as honey or sugar.

Instructions:

1. Peel and chop a ripe mango into small pieces.

2. In a blender, add the chopped mango, 1 cup of coconut milk, and a handful of ice cubes.

3. If desired, add sweetener such as honey or sugar to taste.

4. Blend the mixture until smooth and creamy.

5. Taste and adjust the sweetness or consistency as needed by adding more sweetener or ice.

6. Pour the Mango Coconut Serenity into a glass and serve chilled.

Raspberry Oatmeal Comfort

Raspberry Oatmeal Comfort include oats, raspberries, milk (or a dairy-free alternative), sweetener (such as honey or maple syrup), and optional toppings like nuts or seeds. Here are the detailed instructions:

1. In a saucepan, bring 1 cup of milk (or dairy-free alternative) to a gentle simmer.

2. Add 1/2 cup of oats to the simmering milk and stir well.

3. Cook the oats over low heat, stirring occasionally, for about 5 minutes or until they reach your desired consistency.

4. While the oats are cooking, mash 1/2 cup of raspberries with a fork until they are slightly broken down.

5. Once the oats are cooked, remove the saucepan from heat and stir in the mashed raspberries.

6. Sweeten the oatmeal to taste with honey or maple syrup, stirring well to incorporate.

7. Serve the Raspberry Oatmeal Comfort in bowls and top with your choice of nuts or seeds, if desired.

The Green Goddess Elixir

The Green Goddess Elixir is a popular drink that is known for its health benefits. The Green Goddess Elixir usually includes ingredients such as:

1. Leafy greens (such as spinach, kale, or parsley) - These provide essential vitamins and minerals.

2. Cucumber - Adds hydration and a refreshing taste.

3. Green apple - Adds a hint of sweetness and antioxidants.

4. Lemon or lime juice - Provides a tangy flavor and vitamin C.

5. Ginger - Adds a spicy kick and has potential health benefits.

6. Water or coconut water - Used as a base to blend all the ingredients together.

Instructions:

1. Wash and prepare all the ingredients by removing any stems or seeds.

2. Add the leafy greens, cucumber, green apple, lemon or lime juice, and ginger to a blender.

3. Pour in water or coconut water to help with blending.

4. Blend everything until smooth and well combined.

5. If desired, you can strain the mixture to remove any pulp or fiber.

6. Serve the Green Goddess Elixir chilled or over ice.

The Berry Protein Bliss is a delicious and nutritious drink that is often enjoyed as a post-workout or meal replacement option. The Berry Protein Bliss includes ingredients such as:

1. Mixed berries (such as strawberries, blueberries, or raspberries) - These provide natural sweetness and antioxidants.

2. Protein powder (such as whey, plant-based, or collagen) - Adds protein to support muscle recovery and satiety.

3. Greek yogurt or almond milk - Provides creaminess and additional protein.

4. Banana - Adds natural sweetness and potassium.

5. Honey or maple syrup (optional) - Can be used to sweeten the drink if desired.

6. Ice cubes - Used to make the drink cold and refreshing.

Instructions:

1. Wash and prepare the berries by removing any stems or leaves.

2. Add the mixed berries, protein powder, Greek yogurt or almond milk, banana, and sweetener (if desired) to a blender.

3. Add a few ice cubes to the blender to make the drink cold.

4. Blend everything until smooth and well combined.

5. If the consistency is too thick, you can add more liquid (Greek yogurt or almond milk) to thin it out.

6. Pour the Berry Protein Bliss into a glass and enjoy!

The Ginger Pear Soother is a delicious and soothing drink. Here are the ingredients and detailed instructions:

Ingredients:

- 1 ripe pear, peeled and chopped

- 1-inch piece of fresh ginger, peeled and grated

- 1 tablespoon honey

- 1 cup water

- Juice of half a lemon

Instructions:

1. In a small saucepan, combine the chopped pear, grated ginger, honey, and water.

2. Bring the mixture to a boil over medium heat, then reduce the heat and let it simmer for about 10 minutes, or until the pear is soft.

3. Remove the saucepan from the heat and let the mixture cool slightly.

4. Once cooled, transfer the mixture to a blender and blend until smooth.

5. Strain the mixture through a fine-mesh sieve to remove any pulp or ginger fibers.

6. Stir in the lemon juice and taste. If desired, you can add more honey for sweetness.

7. Pour the Ginger Pear Soother into a glass and serve warm.

Protein-Packed Main Courses

A crucial aspect of post-operative recovery after a hysterectomy is ensuring that your body receives the essential nutrients it needs. This collection of protein-packed main courses has been thoughtfully curated to aid in your healing journey. These recipes are not only rich in protein but also designed to be gentle on the digestive system, providing the sustenance required for a healthy recovery.

Baked Lemon Herb Salmon:

Ingredients:

- 1 pound salmon fillet

- 2 tablespoons olive oil

- 2 cloves garlic, minced

- 1 tablespoon fresh lemon juice

- 1 teaspoon dried dill

- 1 teaspoon dried parsley

- Salt and pepper, to taste

- Lemon slices, for garnish

Instructions:

1. Preheat your oven to 400°F (200°C) and line a baking sheet with parchment paper.

2. Place the salmon fillet on the prepared baking sheet.

3. In a small bowl, mix together the olive oil, minced garlic, lemon juice, dried dill, dried parsley, salt, and pepper.

4. Drizzle the mixture over the salmon fillet, making sure to coat it evenly.

5. Place lemon slices on top of the salmon for added flavor and garnish.

6. Bake the salmon in the preheated oven for about 12-15 minutes, or until it flakes easily with a fork and is cooked to your desired doneness.

7. Once cooked, remove the salmon from the oven and let it rest for a few minutes before serving.

8. Serve the Baked Lemon Herb Salmon with your favorite side dishes and enjoy!

Quinoa and Black Bean Stuffed Bell Peppers:

Ingredients:

- 4 bell peppers (any color)

- 1 cup cooked quinoa

- 1 cup black beans (canned or cooked)

- 1/2 cup corn kernels

- 1/2 cup diced tomatoes

- 1/2 cup diced onion

- 1/2 cup shredded cheese (optional)

- 1 tablespoon olive oil

- 1 teaspoon cumin

- 1 teaspoon paprika

- Salt and pepper to taste

- Fresh cilantro or parsley for garnish (optional)

Instructions:

1. Preheat your oven to 375°F (190°C).

2. Cut the tops off the bell peppers and remove the seeds and membranes. Set aside.

3. In a large skillet, heat the olive oil over medium heat.

4. Add the diced onion and cook until translucent, about 5 minutes.

5. Add the corn kernels, diced tomatoes, cooked quinoa, and black beans to the skillet. Stir well to combine.

6. Season the mixture with cumin, paprika, salt, and pepper. Adjust the seasoning according to your taste.

7. Cook the mixture for another 5 minutes, allowing the flavors to meld together.

8. Stuff each bell pepper with the quinoa and black bean mixture, pressing it down gently.

9. Place the stuffed bell peppers in a baking dish and cover with foil.

10. Bake in the preheated oven for 25-30 minutes, or until the bell peppers are tender.

11. If desired, remove the foil and sprinkle shredded cheese on top of each stuffed bell pepper. Return to the oven for an additional 5 minutes, or until the cheese is melted and bubbly.

12. Remove from the oven and let the stuffed bell peppers cool for a few minutes.

13. Garnish with fresh cilantro or parsley, if desired, and serve hot.

Grilled Chicken and Vegetable Skewers:

Ingredients:

- 2 boneless, skinless chicken breasts

- 1 red bell pepper

- 1 green bell pepper

- 1 yellow bell pepper

- 1 red onion

- 8-10 cherry tomatoes

- 2 tablespoons olive oil

- 2 tablespoons lemon juice

- 2 cloves garlic, minced

- 1 teaspoon dried oregano

- Salt and pepper to taste

- Skewers

Instructions:

1. Cut the chicken breasts into bite-sized pieces and set aside.

2. Cut the bell peppers and red onion into chunks of similar size.

3. Thread the chicken, bell peppers, red onion, and cherry tomatoes onto the skewers, alternating between ingredients.

4. In a small bowl, whisk together the olive oil, lemon juice, minced garlic, dried oregano, salt, and pepper.

5. Brush the marinade over the skewers, making sure to coat all sides.

6. Preheat your grill to medium-high heat.

7. Place the skewers on the grill and cook for about 10-12 minutes, turning occasionally, until

the chicken is cooked through and the vegetables are tender.

8. Remove the skewers from the grill and let them rest for a few minutes before serving.

9. Serve the grilled chicken and vegetable skewers hot and enjoy!

Lentil and Vegetable Stir-Fry:

Ingredients:

- 1 cup lentils

- 2 cups water or vegetable broth

- 1 tablespoon olive oil

- 1 onion, diced

- 2 cloves garlic, minced

- 1 bell pepper, sliced

- 1 zucchini, sliced

- 1 carrot, sliced

- 1 cup broccoli florets

- 1 cup snap peas

- 2 tablespoons soy sauce

- 1 tablespoon rice vinegar

- 1 teaspoon sesame oil

- Salt and pepper to taste

Instructions:

1. Rinse the lentils under cold water and drain.

2. In a medium-sized pot, bring the water or vegetable broth to a boil. Add the lentils and reduce the heat to low. Simmer for about 15-20 minutes or until the lentils are tender. Drain any excess liquid and set aside.

3. In a large skillet or wok, heat the olive oil over medium heat. Add the diced onion and minced garlic and sauté until fragrant and translucent.

4. Add the sliced bell pepper, zucchini, carrot, broccoli florets, and snap peas to the skillet. Stir-fry for about 5-7 minutes or until the vegetables are crisp-tender.

5. In a small bowl, whisk together the soy sauce, rice vinegar, sesame oil, salt, and pepper.

6. Pour the sauce over the vegetables in the skillet and stir to coat evenly.

7. Add the cooked lentils to the skillet and stir-fry for an additional 2-3 minutes to heat through.

8. Remove from heat and serve the lentil and vegetable stir-fry hot.

Tofu and Vegetable Curry:

Ingredients:

- 1 block of tofu, cubed

- 1 tablespoon vegetable oil

- 1 onion, diced

- 2 cloves of garlic, minced

- 1 tablespoon curry powder

- 1 teaspoon turmeric

- 1 teaspoon cumin

- 1 teaspoon coriander

- 1 can of coconut milk

- 1 cup vegetable broth

- 2 cups mixed vegetables (such as bell peppers, carrots, peas, and broccoli)

- Salt and pepper to taste

- Fresh cilantro for garnish (optional)

Instructions:

1. Heat the vegetable oil in a large pan or skillet over medium heat.

2. Add the diced onion and minced garlic to the pan and sauté until the onion is translucent.

3. Add the cubed tofu to the pan and cook until it is lightly browned on all sides.

4. In a small bowl, mix together the curry powder, turmeric, cumin, and coriander. Add this spice mixture to the pan and stir well to coat the tofu and onions.

5. Pour in the coconut milk and vegetable broth, and bring the mixture to a simmer.

6. Add the mixed vegetables to the pan and stir to combine. Cook for about 10-15 minutes, or until the vegetables are tender.

7. Season with salt and pepper to taste.

8. Serve the tofu and vegetable curry over rice or with naan bread.

9. Garnish with fresh cilantro, if desired.

Shrimp and Avocado Salad:

Ingredients:

- 1 pound shrimp, peeled and deveined

- 2 avocados, diced

- 1 cup cherry tomatoes, halved

- 1/4 cup red onion, thinly sliced

- 1/4 cup fresh cilantro, chopped

- Juice of 1 lime

- 2 tablespoons olive oil

- Salt and pepper to taste

Instructions:

1. Bring a pot of water to a boil and add the shrimp. Cook for about 2-3 minutes, or until the shrimp are pink and cooked through. Drain and set aside.

2. In a large bowl, combine the diced avocados, cherry tomatoes, red onion, and fresh cilantro.

3. In a small bowl, whisk together the lime juice, olive oil, salt, and pepper.

4. Add the cooked shrimp to the bowl of avocado and tomato mixture, then pour the dressing over the top.

5. Gently toss everything together until well combined.

6. Taste and adjust the seasoning if needed.

7. Serve the shrimp and avocado salad chilled.

Turkey and Sweet Potato Hash:

Ingredients:

- 1 pound ground turkey

- 2 medium sweet potatoes, peeled and diced

- 1 bell pepper, diced

- 1 onion, diced

- 2 cloves of garlic, minced

- 1 teaspoon paprika

- 1/2 teaspoon dried thyme

- Salt and pepper to taste

- Olive oil for cooking

Instructions:

1. Heat a large skillet over medium heat and add a drizzle of olive oil.

2. Add the ground turkey to the skillet and cook until browned, breaking it up into small pieces with a spatula.

3. Once the turkey is cooked, remove it from the skillet and set it aside.

4. In the same skillet, add a little more olive oil if needed, then add the diced sweet potatoes. Cook for about 5 minutes, stirring occasionally, until they start to soften.

5. Add the diced bell pepper, onion, and minced garlic to the skillet with the sweet potatoes. Cook for another 5 minutes, or until the vegetables are tender.

6. Return the cooked ground turkey to the skillet with the vegetables.

7. Sprinkle the paprika, dried thyme, salt, and pepper over the mixture. Stir well to combine all the ingredients.

8. Continue cooking for another 5 minutes, or until everything is heated through and the flavors have melded together.

9. Taste and adjust the seasoning if needed.

10. Serve the Turkey and Sweet Potato Hash hot and enjoy!

Salmon and Asparagus Foil Packets:

Ingredients:

- 2 salmon fillets

- 1 bunch of asparagus, trimmed

- 1 lemon, sliced

- 2 cloves of garlic, minced

- Salt and pepper to taste

- Olive oil for drizzling

Instructions:

1. Preheat your oven to 400°F (200°C).

2. Cut two large pieces of aluminum foil, enough to wrap each salmon fillet and asparagus.

3. Place one salmon fillet in the center of each piece of foil.

4. Arrange the trimmed asparagus around the salmon fillets.

5. Sprinkle minced garlic over the salmon and asparagus.

6. Season with salt and pepper to taste.

7. Place a few slices of lemon on top of each salmon fillet.

8. Drizzle olive oil over the salmon and asparagus.

9. Fold the foil over the salmon and asparagus, sealing the edges to create a packet.

10. Place the foil packets on a baking sheet and bake in the preheated oven for about 15-20 minutes, or until the salmon is cooked through and the asparagus is tender.

11. Carefully open the foil packets, being cautious of the hot steam.

12. Serve the Salmon and Asparagus Foil Packets hot and enjoy!

Mushroom and Spinach Omelette:

Ingredients:

- 2 large eggs

- 1 cup sliced mushrooms

- 1 cup fresh spinach leaves

- 1/4 cup shredded cheese (optional)

- Salt and pepper to taste

- 1 tablespoon olive oil

Instructions:

1. Heat the olive oil in a non-stick skillet over medium heat.

2. Add the sliced mushrooms to the skillet and sauté them until they are golden brown and tender.

3. Once the mushrooms are cooked, add the fresh spinach leaves to the skillet and cook until they are wilted.

4. In a separate bowl, whisk the eggs together with salt and pepper.

5. Pour the whisked eggs into the skillet with the mushrooms and spinach.

6. Allow the omelette to cook for a few minutes until the edges start to set.

7. If desired, sprinkle the shredded cheese on top of the omelette.

8. Gently fold the omelette in half using a spatula.

9. Cook for another minute or two until the cheese is melted and the omelette is cooked through.

10. Remove the omelette from the skillet and serve hot.

CHAPTER 5

Building a Post-Hysterectomy Diet Plan

Embarking on the journey of recovery after a hysterectomy requires a thoughtful and nourishing approach to your diet. Crafting a post-hysterectomy diet plan involves selecting foods that aid healing, provide essential nutrients, and support overall well-being. In this section, we delve into the key elements of building a post-hysterectomy diet plan, ensuring you have the tools to nurture your body during this crucial phase.

1. Emphasize Protein-Rich Foods:

   - Lean meats (chicken, turkey, fish) provide essential amino acids crucial for tissue repair.

   - Plant-based proteins (tofu, legumes, lentils) offer alternatives for those on vegetarian or vegan diets.

2. Incorporate Healthy Fats:

   - Avocados, nuts, seeds, and olive oil contribute healthy fats that aid in nutrient absorption and provide energy.

   - Omega-3 fatty acids found in fatty fish (salmon, mackerel) and flaxseeds have anti-inflammatory properties.

3. Include Whole Grains:

- Opt for whole grains such as brown rice, quinoa, and oats for sustained energy and dietary fiber.

- These grains aid digestion and support overall gastrointestinal health.

4. Load Up on Fruits and Vegetables:

- Colorful fruits and vegetables are rich in vitamins, minerals, and antioxidants.

- These components aid in reducing inflammation, boosting the immune system, and supporting the healing process.

5. Choose Dairy or Dairy Alternatives:

- Incorporate sources of calcium for bone health, such as dairy products, fortified plant-based milk, and leafy greens.

- Adequate calcium intake is crucial, especially post-hysterectomy, to maintain bone density.

6. Prioritize Hydration:

- Stay well-hydrated with water, herbal teas, and broths.

- Proper hydration is essential for healing, supports digestion, and helps eliminate toxins from the body.

7. Mindful Meal Timing:

- Plan smaller, more frequent meals to prevent digestive discomfort.

- Include snacks that combine protein and healthy fats for sustained energy throughout the day.

8. Limit Processed and Sugary Foods:

- Minimize intake of processed foods, sugary snacks, and refined carbohydrates.

- These foods can contribute to inflammation and may hinder the recovery process.

9. Incorporate Healing Herbs and Spices:

- Ginger and turmeric have anti-inflammatory properties and can be added to soups, smoothies, or teas.

- Fresh herbs like mint, basil, and cilantro not only enhance flavor but also provide additional nutrients.

10. Consider Individual Preferences and Restrictions:

   - Tailor your diet plan to suit your individual preferences, dietary restrictions, and any specific recommendations from your healthcare provider.

   - Ensure you meet your nutritional needs while enjoying a variety of foods that support your recovery.

Sample Post-Hysterectomy Day Meal Plan:

Breakfast:

- Scrambled eggs with spinach and feta

- Whole grain toast

- Fresh fruit (e.g., berries or citrus)

Mid-Morning Snack:

- Greek yogurt with a sprinkle of chia seeds

- Handful of almonds

Lunch:

- Grilled chicken or tofu salad with mixed greens, cherry tomatoes, and avocado

- Quinoa or brown rice on the side

- Herbal tea or infused water for hydration

Afternoon Snack:

- Sliced apple with almond butter

- Herbal tea or water with a squeeze of lemon

Dinner:

- Baked salmon or lentil stew with vegetables

- Sweet potato or cauliflower mash

- Steamed broccoli or asparagus

Evening Snack (if needed):

- Cottage cheese with pineapple

- Chamomile tea for relaxation

Conclusion

Your Nourishing Journey After Hysterectomy

As we reach the final pages of "A Complete Guide to Hysterectomy Recovery and Cooking" it's our sincere hope that this culinary guide has provided not just recipes but a road map for your post-hysterectomy journey. The decision to undergo a hysterectomy is a significant step, and the recovery process is an equally important phase that demands attention to both physical and emotional well-being.

In these pages, we've sought to create more than just a collection of recipes. We've crafted a companion that understands the nuances of recovery, appreciates the importance of nutrition, and recognizes the healing power of food. Your post-hysterectomy experience is unique, and so is your relationship with the meals that fuel your recovery.

Through nourishing recipes designed for both pre and post-operative care, we aimed to offer more than sustenance; we aimed to provide comfort, support, and a sense of empowerment. Each ingredient, each meal, and each note within these pages is dedicated to helping you navigate this transformative period with grace and strength.

Remember, the essence of this cookbook lies not only in the flavors on your plate but in the care with which you approach your post-hysterectomy nourishment. Listen to your body, honor its needs, and relish the healing power of wholesome, thoughtfully prepared meals.

As you savor the delicious concoctions from these pages, may you find solace, strength, and a renewed sense of well-being. Your post-hysterectomy journey is not just about recovery; it's about embracing a new chapter with resilience and embracing the joy of nourishing yourself in every possible way.

Wishing you a journey filled with delicious healing, newfound vitality, and a profound sense of self-care. Bon appétit and may your post-hysterectomy days be filled with health, happiness, and a table abundant with the goodness of life.

Printed in Dunstable, United Kingdom